Miyamoto Musashi: The Life and Legacy of Japan's Most Legendary Samurai

By Charles River Editors

A woodblock print of Musashi by Utagawa Kuniyoshi

About Charles River Editors

Charles River Editors is a boutique digital publishing company, specializing in bringing history back to life with educational and engaging books on a wide range of topics. Keep up to date with our new and free offerings with this 5 second sign up on our weekly mailing list, and visit Our Kindle Author Page to see other recently published Kindle titles.

We make these books for you and always want to know our readers' opinions, so we encourage you to leave reviews and look forward to publishing new and exciting titles each week.

Introduction

Utagawa Kuniyoshi's print of Musashi having his fortune told

"Study strategy over the years and achieve the spirit of the warrior. Today is victory over yourself of yesterday; tomorrow is your victory over lesser men." – Miyamoto Musashi

Samurai Sasaki Kojiro was growing increasingly impatient as he waited on the beach at Funa Island in Kokura. An undefeated master swordsman, he was tense and his anger was getting the better of him. He was on the small island for a duel, a clash of steel between two swordsmen where a man's life could end in seconds. The duel was the ultimate test of the swordsman, and Sasaki, one of the best in Japan, was known as "The Demon of the Western Provinces." However, the Sasaki on the beach did not resemble the fierce warrior of his reputation as he paced back and forth, frustrated by the tardiness of his opponent: the enigmatic Miyamoto Musashi.

Sasaki knew nothing about Musashi except that the mysterious swordsman was undefeated, because aside from that, little was known about Musashi's style or lineage. Although Musashi did have a reputation for keeping a rather unkempt appearance and an unpredictable personality, the mysterious swordsman also was the subject of conflicting stories about his courage and prowess.

Despite all these details (or lack thereof), Sasaki looked forward to the duel since a victory against an undefeated swordsman would only heighten his reputation and increase his chances for an official position within the infamous Hosokawa Clan. Sasaki Kojiro had a distinct fighting style known as "Turning Swallow Cut," a swift and efficient strike named after the motion of the swallow bird's tail in flight. Sasaki had been a professional warrior all is life and had been training in the art of the sword since his youth. Many warriors had been on the receiving end of his technique, which a contemporary described in vivid detail: "His sword seemed to first arc down and then suddenly turn upward like a swallow in graceful and acrobatic flight." Sasaki was also immensely proud of his long sword, which he named Drying Pole.

Though he was understandably confident, Sasaki did not underestimate his opponent, who finally arrived to the island on a small boat. Sasaki noticed something shocking: Musashi did not bring a sword. Instead Musashi, who appeared as if he had just rolled out of bed, brought a wooden oar carved into a makeshift sword as his dueling weapon. Sasaki was furious, and though he was beyond insulted, he drew his sword and prepared to fight to the death. The duel between the two masters thus began with one of them having no sword at all.

Little may have been known about Musashi at the time, but centuries later, he is the most infamous and renowned warrior in Japanese history. As a veteran of the Battle of Sekigahara (1600), Naiwa (1615), and the Shimabara Rebellion in Hizen (1637-1638), Musashi was a seasoned battlefield soldier, went undefeated in over 60 duels, and authored an essential book on strategy, *Go Rin No Sho* (*The Book of Five Rings*). He invented a swordsmanship style called Hi-no-shita Kaizan Shimmei Miyamoto Musashi Masana-ryu, a two sword style that some historians think Musashi may have come up with after being influenced by the two-handed drumming of Japanese drummers. His style has continued to be an influence on the practice of kendo into the modern era.

Adding to his legend was the fact that Musashi did not look like a typical samurai warrior. He was widely reported to have never bathed, never washed his hair, and did present himself like a man with a position in the ruling samurai class. This man, considered to be Japan's finest swordsman, looked more like a wandering vagabond than an elegant, aristocratic warrior. The typical samurai employed by *daimyo*s were expected to be properly dressed and groomed, with clean clothes and neatly cut hair. Some samurai even applied rouge to their cheeks to appear healthy and ready to die for their lords.

Musashi, on the other hand, seemed to have appeared out of thin air, claiming no famous teacher, school, or lineage. He also never entered long term service with a *daimyo*, married, or settled down (although he did serve a number of different prestigious clans). Instead, he wandered throughout the island of Japan as a free spirit, apparently valuing observation and intuition far above technique. Shockingly, he also rarely used a real sword - while he respected the sword, he was not beholden to it and often used whatever was available to duel an opponent. In the same vein, he taught his own students to avoid preferences or to rely on any one tool. Put simply, Musashi was a Japanese warrior like no other.

Miyamoto Musashi: The Life and Legacy of Japan's Most Legendary Samurai chronicles the remarkable life, career, and stories about Musashi and his swordsmanship. Along with pictures depicting important people, places, and events, you will learn about the Musashi like never before.

Musashi's Early Years and First Duel

"Timing is important in dancing and pipe or string music, for they are in rhythm only if timing is good. Timing and rhythm are also involved in the military arts, shooting bows and guns, and riding horses. In all skills and abilities there is timing...There is timing in the whole life of the warrior, in his thriving and declining, in his harmony and discord. Similarly, there is timing in the Way of the merchant, in the rise and fall of capital. All things entail rising and falling timing. You must be able to discern this. In strategy there are various timing considerations. From the outset you must know the applicable timing and the inapplicable timing, and from among the large and small things and the fast and slow timings find the relevant timing, first seeing the distance timing and the background timing. This is the main thing in strategy. It is especially important to know the background timing, otherwise your strategy will become uncertain." – Musashi, *The Book of Five Rings*

Most historians believe Musashi was born in either the village of Sakushu or Banshu in 1584,[1] and the public perception and legend about Musashi's background is that he was mostly a self-taught martial artist. Some scholars still consider this entirely unrealistic, as Musashi's various skills seem "to cover an area of technique that is too vast, too well systematized, and too thoroughly elaborated to have been developed through the experience and thought of a single person."[2] Instead, those historians believe that Musashi received extensive training at an existing sword fighting school, which gave him the foundation from which he built his own distinct fighting style.

It is generally accepted that Musashi's father was Hirata Munisai, a retainer for a *daimyo* in Sakushu, west of Kyoto, but it is thought by some historians that Hirata was not his birth father and Musashi was in fact adopted when he was 9-years-old. Hirata was a skilled fighter in a variety of weapons, including swords and the *jitte*, a metal truncheon equipped with hooks to parry sword blows.[3] An instructor for the Shinmen Clan, Munisai was also a master of jiu jitsu and the use of armor in fighting.[4] He was well-known for his elite skill in the Tori-ryu school of swordsmanship, and given his father's background, Musashi would have been exposed to a variety of martial arts and likely received first-hand instruction from his father at a young age.

---

[1] Tokitsu, 7.
[2] Tokitsu, 7.
[3] Tokitsu, 8.
[4] Wilson, 13.

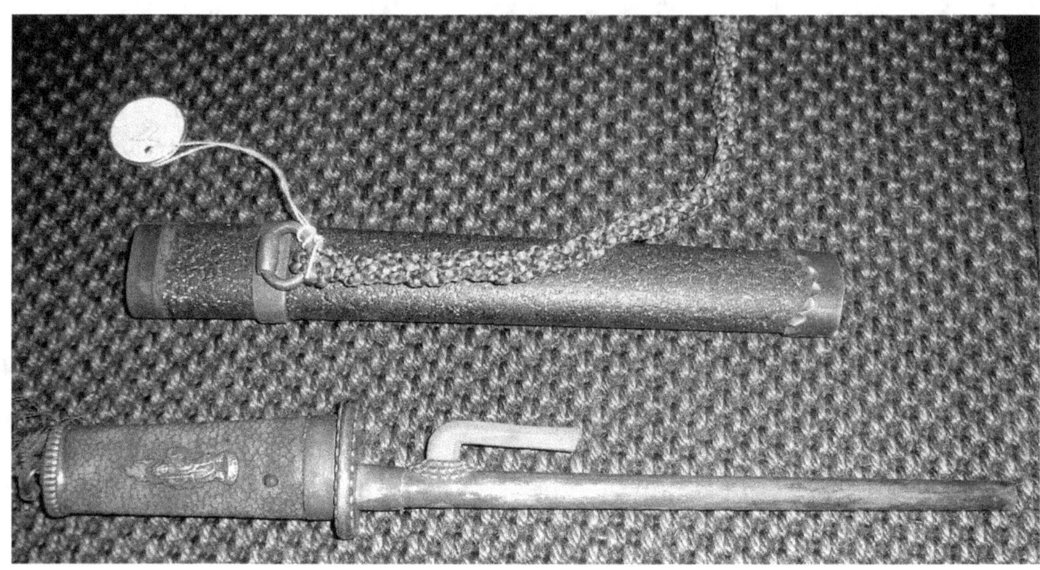

A *jitte* and its case

Although he apparently took such lessons to heart, Musashi did not seem to have a happy childhood. Shortly after Musashi was born, Munisai divorced Musashi's mother and remarried, and the new stepmother did not appear to have gotten along with Musashi. There were also rumors circulating that Musashi's mother was not his real mother.[5] Whatever the case, by the time Musashi was 8-years-old, his relationship with his father had reached such a low point that the young warrior often left to visit his mother, splitting his time between his parents. It was also at this time that Musashi began to receive formal education at the hands of his uncle, the priest Dorin.

A story that best illustrates the faltering relationship between Musashi and his father was relayed: "Bennosuke watched his father's martial arts from the time he was quite young. As he got older, he gradually started to voice critical remarks. Munisai began to think that this child was not very likeable, despite the fact that he was his own son. One day, while Munisai was carving a toothpick, his son approached and began criticizing his jitte technique. Angered, Munisai took the dagger he was using to carve the toothpick, and threw it at his son as though it were a shuriken. Bennosuke dodged the weapon and it lodged in the pillar behind him. Munisai became all the angrier, took his short sword and used it too as a shuriken. Bennosuke dodged this as well and fled outside. After this, he never returned to the house but, rather, lived with a priest related to his mother in Banshu. Thus, he abandoned his hometown."[6]

This rather absurd incident of a grown man attacking his preteen son with lethal weapons represented a turning point in Musashi's life. Musashi now considered Hirafuku, his mother's residence, to be his real home (this is probably the reason why he wrote in *The Book of Five*

---

[5] Wilson, 13.
[6] Wilson, 14.

Rings, "I am a warrior born in Harima.").[7] It was here that Musashi grew into an adult.

Even at a young age, Musashi was notorious for embodying the homeless, ascetic life of a wandering *shugyosha*. He started this journey at the age of 16 and kept up with it until his death. As a result, he owned few possessions, including the simple clothes on his back, a bamboo canteen, a handful of coins, writing brush, and sword.[8] He lived a life of a wandering traveler, straw sandals on his feet and eating whatever he could obtain or afford during life on the road.

Musashi's first duel occurred when he was still just 13, and it was fought against the warrior Arima Kihei, a student of the Shinto ryu school founded by Tsukahara Bokuden (1489-1571). Bokuden was a sword master from the Kashima school, which was a famous school throughout Japan. Musashi himself wrote of the school, "Some time ago, the Shinto priests of the Kantori shrine near Kashima...founded a school, saying that their art had been transmitted to them by the gods, and they propagated this art in all the provinces."[9]

In 1596, Arima was traveling throughout Japan on a quest to perfect his sword skills. Stopping at the village of Hirafuku-mura, Arima posted a public challenge that read, "He who wishes to fight me with the sword should write his name and the date of the duel on this notice board."[10] Musashi saw this challenge and painted the announcement black and wrote his name, address and date, directly challenging the adult warrior to a duel before returning to his residence at his uncle's temple. When he came home to Dorin's temple, Musashi mentioned his challenge to no one; instead, the boy took a piece of firewood and started to carve a wooden sword. A messenger arrived later and said to Dorin, "I have come to convey a message from Arima Kihei, who is traveling to improve his swordsmanship. Would you be kind enough to pass on to Mr. Miyamoto Bennosuke that Arima agrees to fight him at the exact time he indicated."[11]

Dorin was shocked. He did not want his teenage nephew fighting a fully trained adult warrior. Desperate, Dorin tried to stop the duel by attempting to persuade the messenger. Pointing to Musashi, who was sitting down, Dorin told him, "We are talking about this little kid here. It is unthinkable for him to fight a duel. Would you be kind enough to go back, please, and ask Mr. Arima to excuse him, given that it was no more than the silly prank of a young kid to dare to mess up his announcement."[12]

The messenger, upon seeing the young Musashi, laughed and replied, "I understand. But in my opinion Arima will not be persuaded even if I give this explanation. I would like you to come with me to his inn and explain to him directly and make your excuses to him. Then I think he

---

[7] Wilson, 14.
[8] Wilson, 14.
[9] Tokitsu, 15.
[10] Tokitsu, 16.
[11] Tokitsu, 16.
[12] Tokitsu, 17.

will accept. Please come with me."[13]

Dorin followed the messenger to the inn where Arima was staying at, but Arima was not an easy man to appease and insisted that the only way to clear the duel was for Musashi to apologize in person at the predetermined duel location. Arima said, "I understand that carrying on with the duel is out of the question. Since the person in question is a child, it is better just to drop the matter. But I am traveling to various regions and no one will believe that my announcement being painted black when I got to Banshu was only a child's prank. My honor is on the line. I request you come with Bennosuke to the place of the duel on the appointed day and explain to the public the reason the duel is not taking place. That will clear away my dishonor."[14]

On the day of the duel, Dorin accompanied Musashi to the location of the duel, and upon seeing Arima, Dorin attempted to apologize. But Musashi was no ordinary 13-year old, and when he saw Arima, he readied his six-foot wooden sword and shouted, "Come on, let's fight!" He then charged the warrior.[15]

Kenji Tokitsu, a modern Japanese historian, described the duel: "He then attacked Arima. The latter drew his *wakizashi* (short sword) and attacked. The master quickly ducked and Arima's sword cut the air and his hand came down on the master's shoulder. The master dove down and put his hand between his opponent's legs and threw him over his shoulder. The moment Arima tried to get up, the master, who had picked up his wooden sword, struck him hard between the eyes. Arima was stunned and was unable to get up quickly, and during this time the master struck him several blows in a row. Arima died and his disciple ran away. The spectators applauded and shouted out loud, but the monk was extremely upset."[16]

Even taking into account that Musashi became Japan's greatest swordsman and Arima was said to be arrogant and a somewhat unskilled warrior, it is still shocking that a 13-year-old was able to kill an adult like that. Some historians believe the young Musashi took on the duel as a direct challenge against his father and school, which could explain why Musashi angrily wrote on Arima's challenge sign with black ink, a loud call to fight.[17] Moreover, despite their age difference, Musashi had advantages against Arima, including the fact Arima might not have realized that the young teen was planning on a duel to the death. By the time the duel had commenced, Musashi held the initiative and was able to deliver the killing stroke.

Arima had placed himself in an unenviable position. Even if he had won, no particular honor or prestige would be gained for the simple fact that his victory would have been achieved against a child. Conversely, Musashi's victory in his first duel marked his transition to adulthood, and for

---

13 Tokitsu, 17.
14 Tokitsu, 17.
15 Tokitsu, 18.
16 Tokitsu, 18.
17 Tokitsu, 20.

the rest of his life, he would dedicate himself to life the road, constantly in pursuit of perfection with the sword.

Combat and the Tokugawa Shogunate

A self-portrait of Miyamato Musashi

"In strategy your spiritual bearing must not be any different from normal. Both in fighting and in everyday life you should be determined though calm." – Musashi, *The Book of Five Rings*

Most of Musashi's warrior life occurred during the Tokugawa era (1600-1868), a period of peace and stability in Japanese history. The Tokugawa shogunate, a military government under control of a shogun (military dictator) and the last feudal government in Japan, brought an end to the constant civil wars and open warfare of the previous two centuries and ruled for nearly 300 years. Given that it was a military government, military service was critically important to one's social status and essential to occupational classification in the Edo period, making it the perfect age for the samurai.

As a feudal government, the Tokugawa shogunate split control of state domains under feudal lords known as *daimyō*. Although given a high degree of autonomy, the *daimyō* were responsible to the shogun to provide "maintenance of armed forces, the protection of the coastline, and attendance on the shogun at appointed times."[18] The maintenance of these functions required a large amount of support from society in general, including merchants, peasants, and artisans, but this system of military governance ensured that the warriors' social status was elevated to a position of high prestige. Thus, samurai held a virtual monopoly not only on military positions, but also administrative positions at both the central and regional levels, and as a symbol of their status, samurais were the only class allowed to carry weapons - a longsword and shortsword - in public.

---

[18]Jaundrill 2016a:4

A group of samurai during the mid-19th century

Despite the samurai class and military's omnipotent status, the samurai during this period were not all proficient fighters. In an era of peace and lack of warfare, the samurai's martial capabilities began to wane in importance to their social status, so even though the Tokugawa shogunate was a military government, most samurai were relegated to performing administrative and constabulary roles. This led to a curious state of affairs in which a samurai warrior's fighting ability was less important than their social status as a warrior ruling class.[19] The identity of a warrior would be separate from his experience on the battlefield for 200 years.

Naturally, this had a profound effect on the concept of military service. First, it was defined by a wider range of definitions compared to samurai classes during the previous warring states' era. While all samurais carried weapons, many of their occupations had nothing to do with actual fighting, and even samurai assigned to military roles spent the majority of their time carrying out functions such as guard or escort duty instead of actual fighting. The second big change was the effect on the martial arts - as the likelihood of combat decreased, samurai martial art schools focused on technical mastery rather than practical fighting ability.[20]

---

[19] For instance, the samurai, Ōtori Keisuke, being promoted to warrior status in 1857 was the result of his translation abilities and not his skills with a sword (Jaundrill, 2016a, p. 4).

[20] Jaundrill 2016c:15

During the wars prior to the establishment of the Tokugawa shogunate, the armies fielded were the largest Japan had ever seen,[21] and commanders utilized infantry in quantities far larger than previous medieval Japanese armies, which were smaller and reliant on cavalry. These massive armies of foot soldiers (*ashigaru*) were heavily armed with bows and matchlock muskets, and the Tokugawa shogunate took advantage of the large-scale control wielded by their generals by transitioning that military organization directly into civilian administration and defense.[22] The result of this emphasis on military rule was that military service became the basis for the shogunate system in Japan.

The samurai, as Japan's warrior class, was the privileged class of Japan, but due to the lack of large armies, the warrior classes also retracted in size, and some samurai found themselves without a lord to serve. These unemployed samurai (*ronin*) became known as *kabuki mono* (crooked people), living on the margins of society and carrying out criminal acts.[23] Most samurai lived in a selected area of castle towns and received a stipend from their *daimyō*.

A samurai's position in society was composed of three components: rank, income, and position. Rank was hereditary and directly related to income and employment opportunities, and the highest-ranked samurai were from families claiming status as field commanders or senior civil administrators. Below these ranks were the mounted warriors, directly retained by the *daimyō*. These samurai held a variety of names, including fief holder (*kyunin*), horse guard (*umamwari*), and common warrior (*heishi/hirazemuri*). These privileged ranks held rights to their surname, sword, and stipend. Below these warriors was the menial class, samurai responsible for domestic functions of the lord's household.[24] Ranks were directly related to positions samurai were able to hold.

Although Tokugawa samurai lived in peaceful times, the number of warriors assigned to military positions was high. There were three main branches of service for samurai: the military apparatus (*bankata*), the management of a *daimyō's* household (*sobakata*), and the administration of a *daimyō*'s holdings (*yakukata*). The military still held the highest number of samurai positions, with more than half of all retainers in the bankata.[25] Military positions were also the most prestigious - the vast majority of highest-ranked samurai served in the bankata, while administrative posts were dominated by lower-ranked samurai.

There were consequences to this particular system of governance that would have a direct impact on the inevitable clash between samurai and modern Japan's new military system. Due to the peace in the Tokugawa period, administrative matters gradually overtook military readiness in terms of importance. Also, since the Tokugawa military was filled with high-ranking samurai,

---

[21] 150,000 men were mustered for the invasion of Korea in 1592 (Jaundrill, 2016, p. 15).

[22] Jaundrill 2016c:16

[23] Jaundrill 2016c:16

[24] Jaundrill 2016c:17

[25] Jaundrill 2016c:17

military reforms enacted in the 19th century would directly impact warriors who benefited most from the old system.

Another key factor of interest during this period was military training. Thanks to the overall peace and lack of warfare in the Tokugawa period, the practice of martial arts was very different than in previous eras. Historically, training large amounts of men to fight efficiently - both individually and in a large group - was the primary focus for military commanders, so instructors who were specialists in swordsmanship and musketry were highly sought after. This included Musashi, Japan's greatest swordsman, and Inadome Sukenao, a master marksman. Military instructors emphasized techniques with practical battlefield effectiveness.[26]

This lasted into the first phase of the Tokugawa period, when the shogunate rule was still unstable, but as Japan settled into peaceful times, these martial arts disciplines evolved to have a different social and cultural function. Instead of combat efficiency, the martial arts began to value artistic expression and individual achievement.[27] Shogun military rule restricted *daimyō* from using their armies without official permission, and samurai were also forbidden to participate in the types of duels conducted by earlier generations of warriors, making it difficult to establish a reputation or hone one's skills in martial arts. As a result, the focus of martial arts was geared toward mastery of fixed forms (*katas*) as a way to progress through a series of ranks, despite the fact many warriors were deeply concerned that samurai fighting skills would atrophy. In an 1841 criticism on the state of the samurai, warrior Torii Yozo argued that the real enemy of the Tokugawa era was the general state of peace. For 200 years, Japan experienced no large wars, leading its warriors to forget their primary missions.

Many samurai reformers viewed practical military training as a sort of moral reform. This sentiment was explained by Motojima Fujidayu, a warrior and expert musket marksman: "Warriors have the good fortune to live in a time of peace; they can eat their fill and wear warm clothing every day. It is as if they have forgotten the depth of their obligation to their country, and that is regrettable. That is why we go hunting in the mountains like this, to brave the elements and travel on treacherous roads. After days and nights of hardship we return home to bathe, prepare proper meals, and sleep peacefully; and for the first time we reflect on how fortunate we are to live in peaceful times. That is why I want warriors to be bastions of the nation (*kokka no kanjō*), never forgetting war even in times of peace (*chi ni ran wo wasurezu*), training their bodies regularly through such activities as hunting - where they may test their skill with a musket against a living thing."[28]

Throughout Japan's medieval era, the island state engaged in a series of wars, and due to the propensity for armed conflict, tactics and weapons were highly advanced. In the early medieval

---

[26] Jaundrill 2016c:18
[27] "[F]rom self-protection to self-perfection" (Jaundrill, 2016c, p. 19).
[28] Jaundrill 2016c:29

period, battles were largely fought with a combination of mounted archers, infantry with *naginata* (a polearm consisting of a sword blade attached to a long spear), and archers on foot.[29] According to historian Karl Friday, these early medieval Japanese battles "tended to be aggregates of lesser combats: melees of archery duels, and brawls between small groups, punctuated by general advances and retreats, and by volleys of arrows launched by bowmen on foot, protected by portable walls of shields."[30]

Battlefield tactics evolved from a contest of the individual skills of mounted warriors to large organized group assaults beginning around the Nanbokucho period (1337-1392). This pivot was in sync with the changing reasons fueling Japanese wars, which now focused on the conquest of vast territories. To accomplish this new mission, generals needed more specialist units able to function as part of a large, organized war machine.[31] These changes in the late medieval period can be summed as "the increased amount of manpower mobilized in battle; [a] strategic shift away from fights between individual champions, to planned collective movements of armies; the rise of strong fortified castles; the emergence of foot soldiers as a significant strike force; and the introduction of firearms."[32]

The result of this constant warfare was the continuous development and adaptation of weaponry, and the infamous samurai swords were no exception. The first Japanese swords, *tsurugi,* or *chokutō* (straight, double-edged blades), were brought into Japan from China during the Kofun period (300-710). From these progenitor blades came a series of Japanese swords. *Tachi,* curved single-edged swords created in the 9th century, gradually became mor epopular as sword forging advanced. Short curved swords, *uchi-katana,* first made an appearance in the 12th century, and these short blades were worn, blade facing upward, through a sash on the waist in comparison to the *tachi,* which were worn, blade down, on the side.[33] Both of these swords were worn together.

By the 14th century, the *uchi-katana* were elongated, called *katana,* and used as both a stabbing and cutting blade. To complement the *katana,* a short sword, called the *wakizashi,* would be inserted in the waist sash, completing the classic, two-sword samurai outfit.

---

[29] Bennett 2015:33
[30] Bennett 2015:33
[31] Bennett 2015:33
[32] Bennett 2015:33
[33] Bennett 2015:33

Medieval depictions of samurai in combat

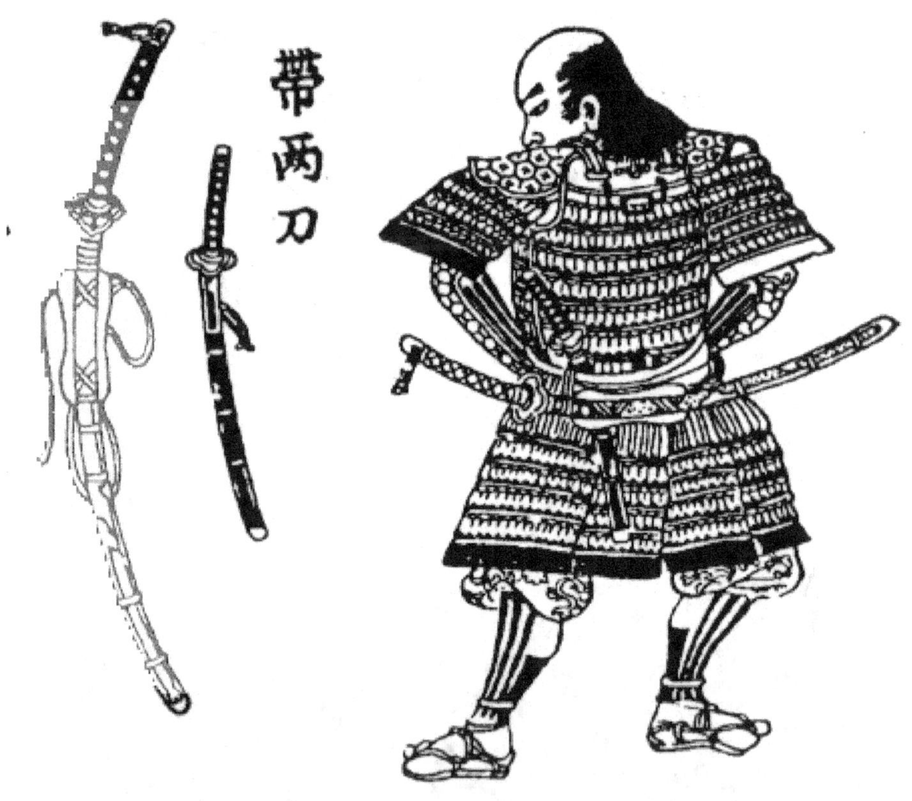

An 18ᵗʰ century depiction of the samurai's weapons

The development of armor in the medieval period also went through several changes. In the early medieval period, samurai warriors wore grand but cumbersome armor, called *ō-yoroi*. This armor had moveable protective panels, giving mounted archers excellent protection and the flexibility to fire arrows at will. This armor came at a cost, however, as foot archers donning the armor were severely hampered and thus had limited maneuverability.[34]

By the late 13th century, this armor had evolved into a cheaper and lighter armor, called *hara-maki*. A big factor for this change in armor was the decrease in the importance of mounted archers. With a simpler and more maneuverable armor, foot soldiers could use long *yari* (spears) with greater efficiency. Swords were also increasing in use – during the late Heian period (794-1185), for example, records show there were 450 swordsmiths, but during the Kamakura period (1185-1333), there were 1,550 swordsmiths. That number ballooned to 3,550 in the Muromachi period (1336-1573).[35]

Despite this increase in the number of swordsmiths, arrows were still a critical battlefield weapon, and a study of battlefield wounds in the Nanbokucho period showed that arrow wounds were still a common form of combat injury. Through a total of 175 documents, historians have identified 554 injuries along with 44 fatalities. One historian noted, "480 (86.6 percent) were caused by arrows; 46 (8.3 percent) by bladed weapons; 15 (2.6 percent) by rocks hurled by sling or rolled from hilltops or fortresses; and 6 [sic] (1.1 percent) by spears."[36]

Based on the widespread damage caused by arrows in battle, it is important to understand the nature of archery in this era, and there were many forms of it. During the Sengoku period (1467-1660), the Ogasawara and Ise families served as the primary instructors for ceremonial archery. This ritualized form was a sport, not only about competition but also about poise and decorum.[37] This form of ceremonial archery was particularly popular among Kyoto's nobility.

Mounted archery was a major factor in medieval combat in Japan and throughout the world. The Mongols had conquered and established the largest empire the world had ever seen on the strength of archers riding on the backs of their steppe ponies.

Mounted archery eventually decreased in popularity with the introduction of firearms,[38] but arrows continued to be used in several ways on the battlefield. During large siege operations, a number of arrows would be fired at both the defenders and the besieged population. On the battlefield, arrows were often fired while musket men reloaded their weapons, and it helped that neither of these conditions required shooting from horseback.[39]

Like sword fighting, the demands and changes on the battlefield determined the archery technique favored by warriors. In the Muromachi period (1336-1573), archers required great speed and penetrating power in combat, so the ceremonial Ogasawara forms were not suitable and did not teach the skills required for contemporary archers in battle. Archery techniques, like other forms of combat, were refined on the battlefield. An example of a ceremonial technique

---

[34] Bennett 2015:34
[35] Bennett 2015:34
[36] Bennett 2015:34
[37] Hurst 1998b:121
[38] Hurst 1998b:121
[39] Hurst 1998b:122

introduced in the late Muromachi period was the *yumigaeri*, which rotated the bow upon releasing the arrow.[40] The yumigaeri technique was not suitable for mounted archery or the battlefield and was, therefore, restricted mostly to sport and ceremonial activities.

Unlike their portrayal in pop culture, samurai actually favored various other weapons instead of their famous swords. As demonstrated by the number of arrow wounds, for much of medieval Japan, projectile weapons were more important than blades on the battlefield. Some scholars have proposed that swords started to gain more usage on the battlefield after the introduction of firearms in the 16th century. This theory argues that since musket balls could penetrate heavy armor, armor-smiths had the incentive to produce a lighter armor,[41] which left the wearers more vulnerable to sword attacks. It also gave the samurai an incentive to close the distance and attack range to reduce the effective firepower of muskets.

On the other hand, some Japanese scholars continue to contest this theory. One Japanese historian, Suzuki Masaya, conducted research on wounds, and he logged "584 wounds in war records from 1563-1600, 263 were inflicted by guns, 126 by arrows, 99 by spears, and 30 by rocks."[42] In these records, Suzuki could only find 40 warriors with sword wounds and 26 killed by blades. Based on this, he theorized that although swords were used in combat, they were probably more useful for the ceremonial *kubi-tori* (removing the heads of the fallen foe, which were cleaned and presented for inspection as "invoices for payment") than actual fighting.[43]

Indeed, as a battlefield weapon, Japanese swords were actually quite vulnerable. According to a katana expert, Naruse Sekanji (1888-1948), blades bent easily when cuts were made at an imprecise angle of trajectory. In the same vein, katanas were prone to snapping when struck on the flat of the blade by spears or staff weapons.[44] Naruse had a great deal of personal experience, having repaired 1,681 blades himself. Out of these swords, 30% had been damaged in duels, while the remaining were due to improper care and haphazard cutting practices.[45] Although these sword limitations did not mean it was an ineffective weapon, it implied that as a free-for-all melee weapon, it did not match the easy to use, robust *yari*. The real value of the sword lay in its use for self-defense in daily life, as well as duels, executions, and assassinations.[46]

Nevertheless, swords reached a level of mystique and ceremonial symbolism among the samurai. The technology to make these iron weapons were imported from China, marking Japan's entry into the Iron Age, and the appearance of the swords also gave them a mystical quality thanks to the shining, hardened steel created with foreign technology. Swords also fulfilled an important function in religious ceremonies, as they were thought to be magical and

---

[40] Hurst 1998b:122
[41] Bennett 2015:34
[42] Bennett 2015:34
[43] Bennett 2015:34
[44] Bennett 2015:35
[45] Bennett 2015:35
[46] Bennett 2015:35

have the power to ward off evil, a belief inherited from ancient Chinese philosophy.

The mystical qualities of the sword helped them became instrumental in many samurai customs. For instance, the term *meitō* was used to refer to a sword with special significance. Swords were believed extraordinary if forged by a legendary smith, belonged to a historical figure, or had an excellent cutting edge.[47]

A lot of samurai gave their legendary blades proper names. Records for sword appraisals are found as early as 1436, during the Muromachi period, an indication that swords represented an owner's authority, giving them status and prestige. Legendary blades were also used as currency - besides being rewarded with land or money, samurai were sometimes rewarded with swords as payment for valor.

Firearms in the form of matchlock arquebuses, known as *espingardas,* first arrived in Japan through the Portuguese.[48] The commonly accepted story of the arrival of firearms in Japan is told in a famous book, *Peregrinations*, written by Portuguese traveler Fernao Mended Pinto (1509-1583). Pinto arrived in Japan in September 1543 aboard a Chinese pirate ship blown off course by a severe storm. Upon arriving, the men were questioned by a local *daimyo*, and a fellow Portuguese traveler demonstrated his arquebus to the *daimyo* by shooting several ducks. The Japanese lord was so impressed that he asked the marksmen to return with him to his castle.[49]

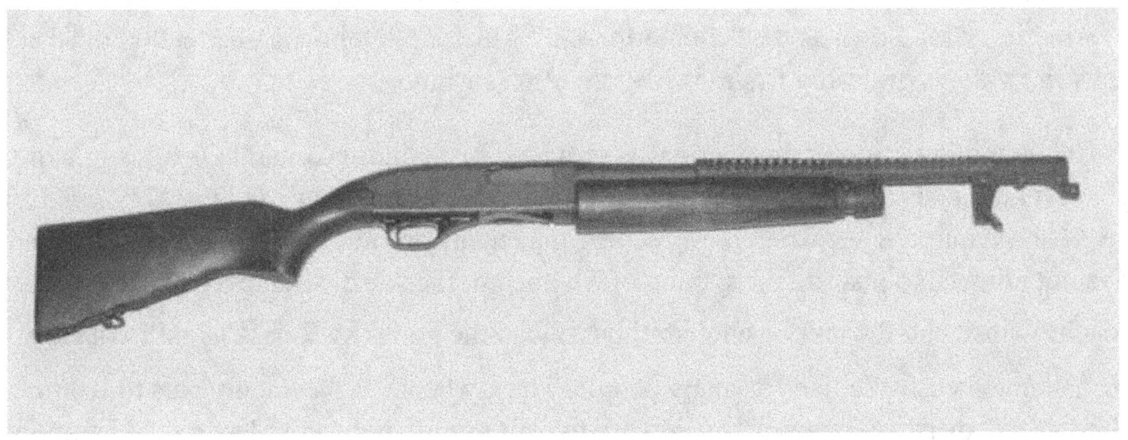

An *espingarda*

There is also a Japanese account of this incident with some notable differences. According to Japanese sources, the Portuguese were asked to demonstrate these curious weapons: "A small white target was set up on a bank…The man gripped the object [i.e., the gun] with one hand, straightened his posture, and squinted with one eye. When thereupon fire issued from the opening, the pellet always hit the target squarely…All bystanders covered their ears."[50] Two of

---

[47] Bennett 2015:36

[48] Andrade 2016:169

[49] Andrade 2016:169

these weapons were purchased by the Japanese and subsequently copied by local smiths.

There is evidence that firearms had arrived in Japan before the Pinto incident, as muskets were in use in Southeast Asia by 1540, where many Japanese had sailed and traveled as mercenaries or merchants. Logic would dictate that some of these weapons would have been brought back to Japan.[51]

Regardless of how firearms arrived in Japan, they were immediately welcomed due to Japan's being engaged in constant warfare. By the early 1580s, about a third of Japan's major armies carried arquebusiers,[52] and by the time the Battle of Sekigahara took place, arquebusiers outnumbered pikemen, archers, and mounted warriors in most armies.

At that time, firearms were the most important infantry weapon for the Japanese armies, so a series of gunnery schools were established, with many of them producing manuals teaching samurai how to shoot from various positions.[53] The Japanese also innovated several battlefield tactics around firearms, one of which was the volley fire. The Portuguese arquebus firearms were guns fired from the shoulder, but while these weapons were quickly adapted by the Japanese and possessed superior power compared to bows, they had a serious flaw: a slow reloading speed.[54] This tactical flaw was addressed by Oda Nobunaga in the 1560s. The warlord realized that by consolidating his troops in lines, he could have the first rank fire a volley and move back to reload while the next rank followed suit, solving the slow reloading problem in a lethal manner. This formation was known as the "countermarch."[55] In 1575, Nobunaga had 3,000 musket men in ranks fire volleys of deadly fire in the Battle of Nagashino.

An excellent description of this tactic was provided by Chinese General Qi Jiguang, who fought several battles against Japanese pirates. In his military manual, *Ji Xiao Xin Shu* (1560), he wrote, "All the musketeers, when they get near the enemy are not allowed to fire early, and they're not allowed to just fire everything off in one go, [because] whenever the enemy then approaches close, there won't be enough time to load the guns (銃裝不及), and frequently this mismanagement costs the lives of many people. Thus, whenever the enemy gets to within a hundred paces' distance, [the musketeers] are to wait until they hear a blast on the bamboo flute, at which they deploy themselves in front of the troops, with each platoon (哨) putting in front one team (隊). [The musketeer team members] wait until they hear their own leader fire a shot, and only then are they allowed to give fire. Each time the trumpet gives a blast, they fire one

---

[50] Andrade 2016:169
[51] Andrade 2016:169
[52] Andrade 2016:170
[53] Parker 2005:60

[54] Parker 2005:60
[55] Parker 2005:60

time, spread out in battle array according to the drilling patterns. If the trumpet keeps blasting without stopping, then they are allowed to fire all together until their fire is exhausted, and it's not necessary [in this case] to divide into layers."[56]

In fact, some historians believe the Europeans learned volley fire from the Japanese. Historian Geoffrey Parker claimed that Nobunaga "devised the idea of the musketry volley some twenty years before it emerged in the west."[57] Parker believed that European observers learned the tactic by watching the Japanese in action, but this theory remains a subject of considerable debate among historians.

Prior to the introduction of firearms, Japanese warfare had consisted of small, independent bands of samurai engaging each other with swords, spears, and arrows. Troops were more prone to fight as individuals rather than cohesively as units in a tactical formation.[58] However, firearms were adopted at a blistering pace by Japan's warlords, and by 1556, more than 300,000 guns were in circulation in Japan.[59] In the beginning, most firearms production was limited to the island of Kyushu, where Portuguese vessels docked for trade, but the manufacture of firearms soon spread elsewhere. Sakai in Izumi Province and Yokkaichi and Kunitomo in Kai Province became areas known for firearms production,[60] and most Japanese military commanders recognized firearms were the most important weapons on the battlefield. Local warlords began to spend more time and resources supplying their forces with an increasing amount of firearms. Takeda Shingen, *daimyo* of Kai Province, addressed his retainers, "Hereafter guns will be the most important [weapons]. Therefore, decrease the number of spears [in your armies] and have your most capable men carry guns. Furthermore, when you assemble your soldiers, test their marksmanship and order that the selection of [gunners] be in accordance with the results [of the test]."[61]

In addition to revolutionizing firearm tactics, the weapons fundamentally changed the nature of other tactics in Japan. Long-range fighting became extremely important as volleys of musket fire were often deadly enough to affect the outcome of a battle before any hand-to-hand fighting could commence. If musket fire was insufficient, arrows, followed by spears and swords, were used,[62] but the focus that armies placed on firearms changed the organization and tactics in Japan. The first major change was the decrease in the cavalry. The importance of mounted warriors declined in importance in Japan throughout the 16th century, which meant infantry became the focal point of Japanese armies. In 1573, an army under Takeda Shingen had one cavalryman for every two infantrymen, but by 1590, Toyotomi Hideyoshi supplied one of his

---

[56] Andrade 2016:173
[57] Andrade 2016:170
[58] Brown 1948:237
[59] Brown 1948:238
[60] Brown 1948:238
[61] Brown 1948:238
[62] Brown 1948:244

armies with only 30 horses.[63] A big factor during this period was that the firearms were not suitable for firing from horseback because they were too cumbersome. This limitation further accelerated the trend toward using foot soldiers over mounted warriors.

The army was also reorganized to accommodate firearms. Musket men were generally placed in the front ranks, followed by companies of archers, and then spearmen and swordsmen.[64] At the center of the army were the commander and his personal group of messengers and retainers, flanked by gunners, archers, and spearmen. Horses and supplies were guarded by infantry, who were positioned in the rear.

The logic behind these formations was focused on harnessing the firepower of the most important battlefield weapon: the musket. Companies of infantry equipped with muskets were placed in the front where they could attack the enemy as soon as they were within range. The archers behind the muskets supported them while the gunners reloaded and repositioned, although at a shorter range.[65] Melee fighters armed with spears and swords were positioned at the front and only fought once the battle descended into hand-to-hand fighting. Japanese armies, therefore, became composed of interrelated units maneuvered into position by generals based on the changing battle circumstances. This required the need for large armies under central control, a factor concentrating military power under the establishment of a single government.[66]

Clever military commanders quickly realized that firearms were especially effective when troops fired behind defensive barriers. At the Battle of Nagashino in 1575, Oda Nobunaga placed his 3,000 musket men behind a series of stockades built on hills opposite enemy camps. Nobunaga sent out small, harassing forces on raids into the enemy's rear, compelling them to launch a frontal attack straight into Nobunaga's musket men. Upon being fired on, the attacking force hoped to press forward and attack before the muskets could be reloaded, but Nobunaga had ordered only 1,000 muskets to fire at a time, and then the next thousand fired while the previous gunners reloaded, thus amassing a constant barrage of fire. The musket fire was devastating, and once the enemy had retreated, Nobunaga ordered his men to leave their barriers and attack in hand-to-hand combat.[67]

Muskets firing from behind defensive barriers became a central battlefield tactic for Japanese warlords in the 16th century. During the Battle of Shizugatake, generals on both sides used defensive musket tactics in which fortified positions consisted of long rows of entrenchments and barricades made from trees. Behind these defenses were towers where "musketeers could play upon the enemy's ranks while at a distance from the entrenchment."[68]

---

[63] Brown 1948:244
[64] Brown 1948:244
[65] Brown 1948:245
[66] Brown 1948:245
[67] Brown 1948:245
[68] Brown 1948:246

Ceremonial Swords

A painting in *The Book of Five Rings* depicting Musashi slaying a giant creature

"Know the smallest things and the biggest things, the shallowest things and the deepest things. As if it were a straight road mapped out on the ground ... These things cannot be explained in detail. From one thing, know ten thousand things. When you attain the Way of strategy there will not be one thing you cannot see. You must study hard." – Musashi, *The Book of Five Rings*

While the use of swords in battle continues to be studied and debated, there is no question that, the sword was always an essential part of a samurai's daily attire. In feudal Japan, the samurai were the only social class authorized to wear the two swords.[69] Although the sword was considered the soul of the samurai spirit to the point of religious reverence, in actuality the sword

---

[69] Hurst, 65.

during this time was more of a symbol of the samurai's high social status in society. The carrying of swords, combined with dress, the distinct samurai hairstyle, and certain class privileges bestowed upon the samurai all separated them from the lower classes of Japanese society. Samurai were even allowed by law to "cut down and discard" (*kirisute gomen*) commoners if they failed to show the proper deference to the elite samurai.[70]

Thus, even if swords were being used in battle on a less frequent basis, swords remained a vital symbol of social status, and even progressive samurai intellectuals like Fukuzawa Yukichi, who stated that "swords were unnecessary in my scheme of things," had no choice but to wear the distinct pair of swords that represented the dress code of his class.[71] It was unthinkable for a Tokugawa samurai to venture outside his house without wearing his swords, regardless of hos well he actually fought with it.

Sword construction during this era of peace declined in quality compared to previous eras due to a lack of actual combat, but the ceremonial decorations of swords reached their highest peak in the Tokugawa era, as did veneration of them.[72] 19th century Englishman Thomas McClatchie, a Japanese expert, noted that "there is no country in the world where the sword has received so much honor and renown as in Japan. Regarded as of divine origin, dear to the general as a symbol of authority, cherished by the samurai as a part of himself, considered by the common people as their protection against violence, how can we wonder to find it called the living soul of the samurai?"[73]

Sword connoisseurship also became an art form, and skilled designers of hilts, scabbards, and sword polishers were able to achieve great fame among the *daimyo* and samurai of Japan. Due to the general peace, the enjoyment and appreciation of the design and art of the sword became more important than the actual use of them to many in Japan.[74] In conjunction with that, since the Tokugawa era samurai were largely inexperienced in the actual realities of combat, they found ways to admire the deadly steel without its connection to the horror, blood and gore of warfare. The connection between the sword with Shinto and Buddhist deities were also strengthened by the dissemination of texts dedicated to the theory and analysis of swordsmanship.[75] Tokugawa texts on martial arts are frequently illustrated with diagrams connecting swords and techniques with the deities from these religions, including Amaterasu, Fudo, Take Mikazuchi no Kami, Hachiman, Marishisonten, and others.[76] These links are often referenced with mystical language employing theories like yin-yang and the five element theory. Thus, swordsmanship grew as a means of self-perfection, which further increased the Tokugawa

---

[70] Hurst, 65.
[71] Hurst, 65.
[72] Hurst, 65.
[73] Hurst, 28.
[74] Hurst, 66.
[75] Hurst, 66.
[76] Hurst, 66.

warrior's identification with their swords as the foundation of their essence. Many samurai viewed the sword as the soul of the warrior or "the mind."[77]

This transformation of the sword, and the manner in which it became the focus of all martial arts during the Tokugawa era, was mentioned in Musashi's work. He explained, "The sword is the basis of *heiho* [martial arts], since it is through the sword that one can pacify both society and oneself."[78]

Of course, it was much easier to come up with theories and religious connections for swords among those who actually had no idea how to use them in a war. During Musashi's life, young boys could learn swordsmanship at one of the many sword fighting schools around Japan. A typical student of these schools would start his training by practicing a series of basic techniques before transitioning to dull metal swords, and then finally graduating to a fully sharpened live sword.[79] Various swords would have been used by these students, such as the long and short sword, with an emphasis on the usage of blades after they were drawn and both fighters "had squared off safely out of striking distance."[80]

By comparison, the second form of swordsmanship, *iai*, focused on the drawing of the sword and cutting in a swift single stroke. Therefore, this technique focused on using blades against sudden attacks within close striking range. Thus, whereas general swordsmanship featured two fighters drawing their weapons out of striking range in a stance before closing in to engage, *iai* swordsmanship was often practiced indoors in close combat range and combined its techniques with unarmed combat such as "throws, pins and joint techniques," which could be used to disarm or prevent the sword draw.[81]

Becoming the *Kensei*

"I have trained in the way of strategy since my youth, and at the age of thirteen I fought a duel for the first time. My opponent was called Arima Kihei, a sword adept of the Shinto ryū, and I defeated him. At the age of sixteen I defeated a powerful adept by the name of Akiyama, who came from Tajima Province. At the age of twenty-one I went up to Kyōtō and fought duels with several adepts of the sword from famous schools, but I never lost." - Musashi, *The Book of Five Rings*

Although Musashi and other samurai did fight in various battles, the general lack of civil war means that duels, with either practice or real swords, were the most important part of training for samurai. Typically, swordsmen would travel alone throughout Japan and seek out well-known

---

[77] Hurst, 66.

[78] Hurst, 66.

[79] John M. Rogers, *Arts of War in Times of Peace. Swordsmanship in Honcho Bugei Shoden, Chapter 6*, (Monumenta Nipponica, vol. 46, no. 2, 1991), 178.

[80] Rogers, 178.

[81] Rogers, 178.

sword masters with the hopes of challenging them to a duel, although they could also be fought for revenge or to uphold honor. These journeys of martial self-improvement were especially popular in the early 17th century, which is why swordsmen like Ito Ittosai participated in 33 duels and Musashi fought a staggering 66.[82]

There were many important aspects that made dueling such a huge component in the life of a swordsman. One critical value of dueling was its ability to enhance the swordsman's fame and reputation as a sword master, to the extent that some swordsmen even traveled with large entourages like modern celebrities. The swordsman Tsukahara Bokuden traveled throughout Japan with an entourage that rivaled a wealthy noble.

Duels were also vital because they were used to decide the successor to a sword master. For example, it was said that the best two disciples of Ito Ittosai competed with each other in duels to see who would assume the title of the sword fighting school after their master.[83] Similarly, these duels between disciples also helped the master determine the skill level of each of his students. Once a student had attained a level equal to that of the master, they were given the award of *inka* (acknowledgement of mastery).[84]

Duels were also often used as demonstrations for high ranking lords. As a swordsman's reputation spread throughout Japan, words of his exploits would reach the ears of various lords, who would summon these talented swordsmen for demonstrations of their skills. During the demonstration, a vassal of the lord would serve as the swordsman's opponent in the match, although at times the swordsman would bring a disciple or a son to serve as the opponent.[85] These weren't duels to the death, and the master swordsmen were not allowed to hurt the vassal - these "duels" were designed to showcase the prodigious skills of the swordsman. A particularly impressive demonstration could greatly elevate the reputation and fame of the swordsman. This fame wasn't strictly for vanity either, because being renowned often brought better career opportunities, like becoming a fencing master for powerful lords.

While the examples cited above were typically used to show off skills, there were plenty of competitive sword matches and tournaments that provided opportunities for fights to the death. For instance, the famous swordsman Kan'ei Joran Jiai had 12 matches organized by the shogun Tokugawa Iemitsu and judged by the shogun's personal fencing masters. This tournament also reportedly took place in the presence of the visiting emperor at the Fukiage Palace in Edo (22nd day, Ninth Month, Kan'ei 11 (1634).[86]

Japanese duels were very different from their European counterparts at the time. Whereas

---

[82] Rogers, 175.
[83] Rogers, 175.
[84] Rogers, 175.
[85] Rogers, 175.
[86] Rogers, 175.

European duelists fought with the same weapons to avoid any unfair advantages, Japanese duelists were usually allowed to utilize any weapon of their own choosing. It was not uncommon for Japanese duels to feature one man armed with a long sword and the other with a *yari*, or a short sword.[87] Even when duels involved wooden weapons, the types could vary, ranging from light bamboo staffs to hardwood clubs enhanced with sharp corners and iron. This was in stark contrast to equivalent European duels, which took extreme measures to ensure that duels remained as equal as possible with identical weapons.

These differences between Japanese and European duels could be analyzed as a fundamental philosophical difference in the concept of fairness. In Europe, duels represented a contest of equal competition, hence the obsession with identical weapons. In Japan, swordsmen using different weapons were seen as fair because it allowed individual duelists to use a weapon that maximized his individual comfort and skill.[88] This Japanese concept of dueling helped bring about the rise of sword masters like Sasaki Kojiro, who utilized his skill in the long sword to his great advantage. Likewise, the Hayashizaki-ryu sword fighting school developed specifically to focus on this long sword technique by lengthening the sword hilt.[89]

Not every sword fighting school held or advocated duels among its students. In fact, some schools even restricted their disciples from engaging in duels until their inka was awarded. This attitude could be found in the early Itto-ryu school, which forbade its members from soliciting duels. However, they were also compelled to accept any challenges issued to them from rival schools.[90]

The most common way to initiate a duel in Japan was to issue an open challenge in a public area by "the best swordsman." All opponents were welcome, and Portuguese Jodo Rodrigues, an interpreter for Hideyoshi and Ieyasu between 1577 and 1610, witnessed many of these duels firsthand: "In the court of Miyako, the capital of Tenka, they [fencing masters] put up a written notice at, for example, the entrance of a main gate in the public square or street of the city where everybody passes by, and it reads: 'So-and-so of such-and-such a place, the most skillful swordsman in all Japan, or Tenka, lives in such-and-such a street or house. Anybody denying this and desiring to challenge him and test him with either real or practice swords, should go and seek him out.' When this has been published and nobody searches him out to challenge him, his claim is confirmed because there was nobody in the capital of Tenka who dared to contradict him."[91]

In 1600, as the war between the Toyotomi and Tokugawa clans was reaching its height, Musashi fought with the Toyotomi Clan since his family owed its allegiance to the Shinmen

---

[87] Rogers, 176.
[88] Rogers, 177.
[89] Rogers, 177.
[90] Rogers, 177.
[91] Rogers, 177.

Clan. He fought in the battle to take Fushimi Castle in July 1600, the defense of Gifu Castle in August 1600, and in the climactic Battle of Sekigahara, which ushered in the Tokugawa shogunate (although there is some doubt on the historical accuracy of Musashi's participation in at Sekigahara).

According to *The Book of Five Rings*, Musashi fought in a total of six battles, but Musashi's most famous exploits would all come in duels, for which he would develop his own unique style. Since Musashi's father was a *jitte* expert, as a child, Musashi learned his father's weapon of choice. He practiced the truncheon seriously, studying it day and night, and through this practice, Musashi soon realized there were many advantages the *jitte* had over the sword.[92] At the same time, Musashi realized that the *jitte* was not a commonly carried weapon compared to the two swords carried everyday by samurai. As a result, by using his unique skills with the *jitte,* Musashi sought to wield the two swords in a way that would utilize the advantages he learned from practicing with the *jitte.* In time, these abilities would allow Musashi to stop using the *jitte* and dedicated himself to a style that relied on two swords, as illustrated by the following passage: "His skill was indeed as exquisite as a sword dance. His steel swords flew; his wooden swords leaped. His opponents ran and dodged, but were unable to escape. He was like an arrow shot from a mighty crossbow. He never missed, and not even Yang You was superior. His hands had mastered swordsmanship and his entire appearance radiated his bravery."[93]

After his victory against Arima Kihei, Musashi would continue his quest to duel and test his sword skills. When he was 16 old in 1599, Musashi left his village and abandoned all his family possessions, leaving them with his sister and her husband.

Musashi's second duel was against an adept named Akiyama in the Tajima Province. Akiyama was a skilled warrior, but like before, Musashi stuck the man dead with as "little effort as it takes to turn one's hand."[94]

Afterwards, Musashi traveled to the capital of Kyoto, where he sought to challenge the Yoshioka-ryu School, known as the best swordsmanship school in Japan. Musashi's father had previously dueled several members of the Yoshioka School, winning two of three in front of the shogun. The Yoshioka School (its lineage could be traced from either the Tenshin Shōden Katori Shintō-ryū or the Kyo-hachi-ryū) was considered the best of the eight major martial arts schools in Kyoto. According to legend, these eight martial arts schools were founded by eight monks on the sacred Mount Kurama. The Yoshioka Clan had fought against the Tokugawa shogun at the Battle of Osaka.

Starting in 1604, Musashi would fight several members of the Yoshioka School. Yoshioka Seijuro, the heir to the school, confronted Musashi on the outskirts of Edo after Musashi had

---

[92] Rogers, 190.
[93] Rogers, 190.
[94] Rogers, 190.

challenged Yoshioka Seijuro to a duel. Yoshioka Seijuro accepted, and they agreed to fight outside Rendaiji in Rakuhoku, in northern Kyoto, on March 8, 1604. Musashi arrived late (a strategy and habit Musashi would employ often), which infuriated Seijuro.

According to one account of the duel, "The two strong men fought fiercely like a dragon and a tiger. With a single blow of Musashi's wooden sword, Yoshioka fell face down and stopped breathing. Since he had fallen with a single blow, Musashi spared him his life. Seijuro's students laid him out on a plank and carried him off. Thanks to medicines and baths at the springs, he gradually recovered. Yoshioka eventually gave up swordsmanship and received the tonsure."[95]

That said, there are many different versions of Musashi's duels, including different accounts of this duel relayed by the same author: "During his match with Yoshioka, Musashi wore a scarlet handcloth as a headband, while Yoshioka wore a white one. Yoshioka's sword grazed Musashi's forehead, Musashi's sword grazed Yoshioka's forehead. Since Yoshioka was wearing a white headband, the blood quickly showed, but as Musashi's headband was scarlet, it was some time before the blood became noticeable. According to yet another version, Yoshioka was younger than twenty and still wore his hair in the fashion of a youth. Accompanied by a single pupil, Yoshioka arrived first at the appointed place. He leaned on his large wooden sword as if it were a cane and awaited Musashi's arrival. Musashi then arrived in a simple litter and stepped out on the side toward the place where Yoshioka was waiting. He removed his two wooden swords from their bag, which he then used to wipe them. Holding a sword in each hand, Musashi advanced. Yoshioka took a stance with his large wooden sword and struck at Musashi. Even though Musashi was able to block it, his headband was knocked off and fluttered to the ground. Musashi dropped to one knee, parried, and with his wooden sword slashed out at Yoshioka's leather hakama. Yoshioka succeeded in knocking off Musashi's headband, Musashi succeeded in ripping Yoshioka's hakama. The spectators were amazed, realizing that here were two master swordsmen and it was impossible to decide who was superior."[96]

With their master defeated, the Yoshioka School was now in the hands of the brother, Yoshioka Denshichirō, who was also a highly skilled swordsman. Seeking revenge, he quickly challenged Musashi to a duel. This sword fight was to take place in Kyoto outside the temple Sanjūsangen-dō.

Denshichirō arrived to the duel armed with a staff fortified with steel rings "more than five shaku in length."[97] Again, Musashi arrived late, and again, his opponent was angry at the tardiness. As the fight started, Musashi was able to disarm the staff from Denshichirō and stuck the man with his own weapon. Denshichirō fell to the ground, dying quickly.

Having suffered a second straight defeat, the Yoshioka Clan was furious. Now, the leadership

---

[95] Rogers, 190.
[96] Rogers, 193-194.
[97] Rogers, 191.

of the family resided in the hands of the 12-year old Yoshioka Matashichiro. Fueled with intense hatred for Musashi as the man responsible for their disgrace, students from the Yoshioka School plotted to have him killed. They mustered a force of archers, musketmen and swordsmen and challenged Musashi to a duel once again on the outskirts of Kyoto. These men justified their schemes of ambushing Musashi by claiming that "strategy allows not meeting the opponent in good faith; an army has to devise plans."[98] However, Musashi must have sensed something was amiss and showed up to the duel location hours early instead of late. Staying hidden, Musashi saw the force assembled against him and attacked. The Yoshioka students were stunned by this lone man charging at them and broke ranks, unnerved by Musashi's solitary assault.

The following description from Musashi's tombstone describes this chaotic fight: "So they met up with Yoshioka Matashichiro at Sagarimatsu on the outskirts of the capital, and several hundred of his students, armed with staffs and bows, went out to do harm to Musashi. Musashi's genius lay in always foreseeing when something was going to happen and he had a talent for knowing when the opportunity was right. He immediately caught on to Yoshioka's deception and told his own students, 'This affair does not concern you directly. You should disperse immediately. What if they form a great crowd or army of enemies full of hatred? I shall watch this as impassively as the floating clouds. Why should I fear them?' Seeing Musashi fearlessly rushing toward them, the mob scattered as if chased by a wild beast, and with their confidence shattered, they returned home. The people of the capital were amazed at this. The bravery, the intelligent strategy that allowed one man to take on a myriad of enemies-truly this was the wondrous principle that lies behind the art of swordsmanship."[99]

Musashi was able to kill Yoshioka Matashichiro and still escape while also fighting off many of his attackers. Legend states that Musashi was forced to draw his second sword and fight with a sword in each hand in order to deal with so many opponents. This marked the start of his *Niten Ichi-ryū* sword style, Musashi's famous two sword style. For Musashi, the second sword was not simply occasionally useful, but essential.

The death of Yoshioka Matashichiro crippled the Yoshioka School, and Musashi's legend grew with his victory over the Yoshioka Clan. People were understandably awed by a single man's ability to defeat so many skilled foes.

---

[98] Rogers, 191.
[99] Rogers, 191.

A monument marking the location where Musashi fought the Yoshioka Clan

Leaving Kyoto, it appears Musashi then traveled to Hozoin in Nara to test himself against the warrior monks, famous for their skill in lance weaponry. Settling down at the Enkoji Temple in Banshu, he would also teach the head monk's brother in the sword. From 1605-1612, Musashi traveled throughout Japan on a *musha shugyo* (warrior pilgrimage) during which he honed his swordsmanship in a series of duels. While most duelists during this era did not try and take their opponent's life unless determined otherwise by both fighters beforehand, Musashi was famous for not being concerned about the type of weapon his opponent used, and he defeated a series of other well-known swordsmen, including the kusarigama practitioner Shishido Baiken. In Edo, Musashi defeated Musō Gonnosuke who would go on to establish the influential staff-fighting school called Shintō Musō-ryū. Legend states that after Muashi defeated him, Muso Gonnosuke dedicated himself to developing a stick-fighting style to directly counter swords and possibly beat Musashi in a rematch.

By the time that Musashi had completed all these duels, his fame as a swordsman had reached legendary status. Perhaps the best description of his awe-inspiring reputation is the inscription on his tombstone:

"Throughout the land, none of these brave and skilled swordsmen can compare. There is only one Musashi. His renown has reached across the four seas and his praises have never ceased to be sung. He truly left a deep impression on even those well versed in such affairs; they agree that he was strange and wondrous, different from any other swordsman. Indeed, Musashi was truly strong and brave.

"Musashi always used to say, 'Swordsmanship is grasped by the mind through practice. If there is no trace left of the self, then surely there is nothing difficult in commanding a great army on the battlefield or ruling a province.'

"During the plot of Toyotomi's treacherous vassal, Ishida Jibu-no-sho, and at the time of Hideyori's insurrections in Osaka and Settsu, Musashi was renowned for his valor and skill with the sword. No matter how flattering the phrase, his greatness cannot be sufficiently lauded; no brief description can do him full justice. He was also well versed in etiquette, music, archery, horsemanship, calligraphy, mathematics, and literature. Highly accomplished in the minor arts, there was virtually nothing he could not do. Truly an amazing man. On his deathbed in Higo, he wrote as his legacy, 'Even though I may die, the great, true, all-embracing art of swordsmanship shall never cease.'

"I, his faithful son, do hereby erect this monument so that his deeds may be known. I can only hope that posterity may deign to read it. Ah, how great a man was he!"[100]

The School of Two Swords

"There is no fast way of wielding the long sword. The long sword should be wielded broadly, and the companion sword closely. This is the first thing to realize. According to this Ichi school, you can win with a long weapon, and yet you can also win with a short weapon. In short, the Way of the Ichi school is the spirit of winning, whatever the weapon and whatever its size." – Musashi, *The Book of Five Rings*

As the sword became more prevalent and the principal weapon of the samurai, several master swordsmen started to codify the best techniques and teach these skills to the next generation of swordsmen. These individual styles and schools are called *ryuha*,[101] and they dominated in Japan from 1500-1700. Initially, many of these masters were able to teach their techniques to their disciples orally (later, in written scrolls). Sword fighting also began to focus on *kata* (forms,

---

[100] Rogers, 192.

[101] Cameron Hurst, *The Early Tradition*, (Armed Martial Arts of Japan: Swordsmanship and Archery, Yale University Press, 1998), 48.

"prescribed movements"), created by masters to be the authoritative technique on sword fighting. Such movements were practiced religiously by the students of their master's school and style.

Many of these sword fighting schools drew influences from Zen Buddhist philosophy and aesthetics. Zen Buddhism places great value on the process, specifically on the performance of the act itself. By creating, or recreating, these forms, the practitioner of these *kata* forms desired to reach a level of self-understanding and enlightenment through the practice of the *katas*.[102] This quest for deeper meaning and enlightenment was practiced not only through sword fighting, but also through calligraphy and flower arrangements. This represented a transformation of martial arts techniques into a philosophical pursuit, and many schools shifted away from pure fighting skills to abstract artistic techniques.

Musashi established a new school centered on his technique using two swords and taught this method to his students. Musashi's two sword school was a very innovative concept at the time since no sword fighting school focused so heavily on the technique of fighting with two blades.[103] Although Musashi explains in *The Book of Five Rings* the reasoning behind the two sword approach, he never provided the origins as to how or why he concluded that using two sowrds was best.

The reasoning behind Musashi's insistence on two swords has been explained in several ways. The first theory is that Musashi realized the benefit of two swords from his childhood in the village. Growing up in the village of Miyamoto, young Musashi would have observed the priests at the Shinto shrine beating the drums for morning and evening prayers.[104] The priests beat the drum with one short stick in each hand. Legend states that Musashi observed these movements and was struck with an epiphany for his style.

Some modern-day kendo practitioners remain skeptical of this origin story. According to Yoshida Seiken, the connection between drums and Musashi is pure myth: "There is no connection whatever between the mind of the School of Two Swords and the fact that the sounds made by a drum are the same whether you strike it with one hand or the other….There is nothing to link the School of Two Swords with the manipulation of two sticks to beat a drum."[105] However, there are others who believe the drum origin story. Morita Monjuro, a kendo practitioner, wrote, "The two drumsticks are big and long. In using them you put forward first one foot, then the other."[106] Trying the drums for himself, Morita realized that the action of beating the drums produced "between the upper and lower limbs, two diagonal tensions that crossed at the level of the lower belly (*tanden*)."[107] Morita realized that this action required

---

[102] Hurst, 48.
[103] Tokitsu, 22.
[104] Tokitsu, 23.
[105] Tokitsu, 23.
[106] Tokitsu, 23.
[107] Tokitsu, 23.

flexibility in the pelvic area, and the striking of the sticks aligned extremely well with Musashi's two sword style.

Although many sword masters and samurai used both swords in battle at different points of the fighting, Musashi's two sword style was unique in that his style advocated using both swords at the same time. Before Musashi's style, samurai would use either their long or short swords depending on the tactical situation because Japanese sword fighters fought with a two-handed sword grip. However, in Musashi's two sword style, he taught the techniques of drawing and holding the sword with one hand. This one-handed grip allowed the fighter to draw both swords at once, a practice that is still being taught in the modern era.

Sasaki Kojiro

"To master the virtue of the long sword is to govern the world and oneself, thus the long sword is the basis of strategy. The principle is "strategy by means of the long sword". If he attains the virtue of the long sword, one man can beat ten men. Just as one man can beat ten, so a hundred men can beat a thousand, and a thousand men can beat ten thousand. In my strategy, one man is the same as ten thousand, so this strategy is the complete warrior's craft." – Musashi, *The Book of Five Rings*

Musashi's most famous duel was fought Sasaki Kojiro (also known as Sasaki Ganryu), a legendary swordsman in his own right who was renowned for his swift and elegant "Turning Swallow Cut." Seeking to enhance his already stellar reputation, Sasaki sought to duel Musashi, and the duel would be to the death with live swords, not practice weapons.

The duel took place on April 13, 1612 at Funa Island, a small island in the waters of Kanmon Straits close to Kokura). On the day of the duel, Sasaki was rowed to the island well ahead of the scheduled duel time. Word of the duel between two master swordsmen had spread throughout the area, and a large crowd of people of all social classes had also traveled to watch the duel. Sasaki noticed this and spoke to his ferryman while he sat on his boat, commenting on the large number of boats in the water. According to an account:

> "He commented to the ferryman on the unusually large number of boats on the water and asked the reason. The man replied, 'Does your lordship not know? Today a swordsman by the name of Ganryu will engage Musashi in a match at Funashima. The boats bringing people hoping to watch have not ceased since before dawn.'

> Sasaki answered, 'I am Ganryu.'

> The ferryman was startled and in a soft voice said, 'If you are Ganryu, then I shall land the boat elsewhere. You must leave quickly for another province. Even though your lordship's skill may be comparable to the gods, Musashi has many followers.

There is no chance that you will leave the island alive.'

Ganryu replied, 'It is as you say. In today's match, I have no hopes that I shall
return alive. But even though you are right, I have made a firm promise to go to the
match, and such is the lot of a brave warrior that not even the fear of death can
allow him to break his promise. I am sure to die on Funashima. I ask that you but
pray for my spirit and pour water on my grave in offering.'

Moved by the ferryman's concern, Ganryu took his purse from the folds of his
robes and presented it to him, although he was of low birth. The ferryman was
reduced to tears by the manly strength shown by Ganryu.[108]

Sasaki arrived on the island and waited for Musashi, who showed up three hours late. At first,
Sasaki was not immediately concerned by his opponent's tardiness, because Musashi was
departing from an area that often experienced rapidly changing currents, so it was not unusual for
a traveler to be late coming from that area. As he waited, perhaps Sasaki thought of the type of
weapon Musashi would use. No one in Sasaki's entourage could be sure what type of weapon
Musashi would bring to the duel, but Sasaki was very proud of his unique long sword, Drying
Pole.[109] A samurai's sword represented his soul, and Japanese warriors took great pride
possessing blades that represented their lineage. In fact, Sasaki represented the perfect ideal of a
master swordsman in the Tokugawa era, as both Sasaki and his teachers came from prestigious
lineages. Through intense training, he became a master and created his own distinct style, which
he then taught at his own sword fighting school. He was next in line to serve as the sword
instructor for the prestigious Hosokawa Clan.[110] In essence, Sasaki had the perfect career and
was the envy of many disciples and swordsmen in Japan.

Legend has it that Musashi had slept past the appointed time of the duel and was so behind that
he even made the manager of his lodging nervous.[111] Meanwhile, having waited for so long,
Sasaki was rapidly losing patience, and when Sasaki saw Musashi's boat approach the beach, he
angrily met the tardy duelist and accused him of disrespect. Musashi did not react.

To seemingly compound matters, Musashi did not bring a sword. Instead, he brought a four-
foot wooden oar carved into a wooden sword,[112] suggesting Musashi had spent the long boat ride
carving the makeshift weapon.

Sasaki was furious and unsheathed his sword and flung the scabbard away into the waves.
Musashi saw this and said, "You've lost, Kojiro. Only the loser will have no need for his

---

[108] Rogers, 192-193.
[109] Wilson, 3.
[110] Wilson, 3.
[111] Wilson, 152.
[112] Wilson, 152.

scabbard."[113]

When the duel started, Sasaki attacked first. The first strike was a feint, with the return strike being the actual attack. This was called a *kaeshiwaza* (returning technique).[114] However, Sasaki did not use his patented technique, the swallow cut, in his final strike. Instead, Sasaki attacked Musashi in a *jodan* position (with his long sword positioned over his head).

It's curious that Sasaki did not use the technique that had won him so many duels, and it has left plenty of people wondering why he changed tactics. It's possible that Musashi's mind games of showing up late and using a wooden sword had rattled Sasaki from his usual confident self. It's also possible that Sasaki was nervous about Musashi's reputation since he had defeated the entire Yoshioka Clan.

With his first attack, Sasaki's blade sliced through Musashi's clothes, coming dangerously close to slaying him, but it was not quite enough. Musashi's struck at the same time and delivered the final blow, crushing Sasaki's chest and killing him.[115]

It is commonly believed that Musashi had carefully planned his late arrival and choice of weapon in a deliberate attempt to throw off Sasaki. Musashi would have been cautious with Sasaki, a skilled warrior. Understanding that Sasaki had a strong sense of classic samurai honor, Musashi knew that his dignity would be thrown off balance by the extremely late appearance of his opponent. He also knew that Sasaki would be deeply offended by Musashi showing up to the duel with such an inappropriate weapon.[116] He knew Sasaki would be impatient having to wait and would be furious at the thought of dueling a warrior armed with a ragtag wooden oar. In the Fire chapter of *The Book of Five Rings* called "Agitating Your Opponent," Musashi wrote, "There are many kinds of agitation. One is a feeling of danger, a second is a feeling that something is beyond your capacity and a third is a feeling of the unexpected. You should investigate this thoroughly."[117] In another section of the chapter, he wrote, "In my martial art...you bend and warp your opponent, taking the victory by twisting and contorting your opponent's mind."[118] It is clear that underneath his disheveled outer appearance of Musashi, a cunning warrior lurked inside, entirely aware of what he was doing.

---

[113] Wilson, 153.
[114] Wilson, 43.
[115] Wilson, 153
[116] Wilson, 153.
[117] Wilson, 153.
[118] Wilson, 153.

A depiction of Musashi (left) dueling Sasaki Kojiro

The Book of Five Rings and Musashi's Legacy

"When I reached thirty I looked back on my past. The previous victories were not due to my having mastered strategy. Perhaps it was natural ability, or the order of heaven, or that other schools' strategy was inferior. After that I studied morning and evening searching for the principle, and came to realize the Way of strategy when I was fifty. Since then I have lived without following any particular Way. Thus with the virtue of strategy I practice many arts and abilities — all things with no teacher. To write this book I did not use the law of Buddha or the teachings of Confucius, neither old war chronicles nor books on martial tactics. I take up my brush to explain the true spirit of this Ichi school as it is mirrored in the Way of heaven and Kwannon. The time is the night of the tenth day of the tenth month, at the hour of the tiger." – Musashi, *The Book of Five Rings*

Musashi had already fought in 60 or more duels by the age of 30, including his first at the age of 13 against Arima Kihei, a Shinto-ryu swordsman, and even though Musashi was victorious in all his duels, he had a rather humble assessment of his abilities. In *The Book of Five Rings*, Musashi confessed that in his opinion, his success could be attributed more to incredible luck rather than overwhelming tactics and skill.[119]

Regardless of whether that was actually true, by the age of 30, Musashi was struck with the sense that he had reached the limit of his physical skills and started to crave a more spiritual connection.[120] Throughout his life, Musashi was credited with a number of works on the subject of martial arts and strategy. These documents include the *Hyōdōkyō* (*The Mirror of the Way of Strategy*), written around 1605, *Hyōhō kaki-tsuke* (*Notes on Strategy*) written around 1638), *Hyōhō sanjūgo-kajō* (*Strategy in Thirty-Five Articles*), written in 1641, and *Dokkōdō* (*The Way to be Followed Alone*), written in 1645.[121]

In 1640, Musashi was invited to be the advisor of the *daimyo* of the Kumamoto domain, Hosokawa Tadatoshi. While in the Kumamoto domain, Musashi lived in a cave and wrote *The Book of Five Rings*, which he completed in 1645, shortly before his death. In fact, *The Book of Five Rings* was passed down to his students so close to his death (about a week) that many historians have theorized his students actually finished the book.[122]

There is also plenty of debate surrounding why Musashi wrote *The Book of Five Rings*. One common theory was that Musashi was dying of a fatal disease and wanted to use what little time he had to transcribe his knowledge to ensure his legacy. Another theory was that Musashi wished to be awarded an official position somewhere, and that this work would help accomplish that goal.[123]

The Book of Five Rings can be broken down into five chapters: Chi (Earth), Sui (Water), Ka (Fire), Fū (Wind), and Kū (Void). The Chi chapter documents the first half of Musashi's life and gives an introduction on tactics and the "metaphysics behind his school," the *Niten Ichi-ryu*, which centered on the strategy of wielding two blades at once.[124] In Sui, he breaks down the various components of individual combat, including mental and physical posture, gaze, footwork, sword techniques, and stances. For the Ka chapter, Musashi dives into the strategy behind choosing an optimal site for dueling, how to control the enemy by seizing the initiative, and other strategic considerations. In Fu, he analyzes the weakness of the other schools of swordsmanship. For the final chapter, Ku, Musashi details his account of how he created his style of fighting, which was heavily influenced by his combat and dueling experiences. His descriptions are philosophical in nature. Musashi refers to the supreme level of combat as the "void" or "emptiness" as it relates to the spirit (things that cannot be seen by the naked eye).[125] In Musashi's opinions, people often mislabel elements they do not understand as unreal and refer to it as emptiness. However, the true void is the "realm of perfect clarity, devoid of delusion, ego, or evil."[126] Without this knowledge of the void, it is impossible for anyone to ascertain what

---

[119] Alexander C. Bennett, *The Art of Living: EARLY MODERN KENJUTSU*, (Kendo: Culture of the Sword, 1st ed., University of California Press, Oakland, 2015), 63.
[120] Bennett, 64.
[121] Bennett, 64.
[122] Bennett, 64.
[123] Wilson, 261.
[124] Bennett, 64.
[125] Bennett, 64.

is truth or not. By understanding this truth, one can understand the "true path" which can be applied to everything from the way of the warrior to a carpenter practicing his craft.[127]

This philosophy makes Musashi unique, as he attributes this truth to all elements of his activities, ranging from armed combat to painting and the arts. He wrote, "If you master the principles of sword, when you freely beat one man, you beat many men in the world. The spirit of defeating a man is the same for ten-million men. The strategist makes small things into big things, like building a great Buddha from a one-foot model. I cannot write in detail how this is done. The principle of strategy is having one thing, to know ten-thousand things."[128]

Although deeply philosophical, Musashi's central thesis in *The Book of Five Rings* is relatively straightforward in comparison to the works of other masters, such as Munenori's *Heihōkadensho*.[129] Musashi also does not include many elements of Zen or Confucian teachings in this philosophy. However, there remains a commonality in those teachings with the mindset that Musashi advocates in combat, specifically on the mastery of strategy as being a never-ending pursuit of perfection that can also be applied to pursuits outside of the martial arts.[130]

Indeed, much of Musashi's fighting philosophy can be traced to his understanding of Zen Buddhism. As a young man, one of Musashi's first lessons on the difference between the aspects of brute strength and courage was when he was captured by the Zen master Takuan, who told him, "In the long run, it doesn't make any difference. You were outwitted and outtalked instead of being outpummeled. When you've lost, you've lost. It would have been crazy of me to try to take you by force. You're too strong physically. It's the same with your so-called courage. Your conduct up till now gives no evidence that it's anything more than animal courage, the kind that has no respect for human values and life. True courage knows fear. It knows how to fear that which should be feared. Honest people value life passionately, they hang on to it like a precious jewel. And they pick the right time and place to surrender it to die with dignity. You were born with physical strength and fortitude, but you lack both knowledge and wisdom…people talk about combing the Way of Learning and the Way of the Samurai, but when properly combined, they aren't two–they're one. Only one Way."[131]

Musashi is considered the most famous swordsman in Japanese history today, but the stories about him spread throughout Japan even when the sword master was still alive. In the villages of Harima and Mimasaka, Musashi became famous after he defeated Arima Kihei. Adding to his fame, Musashi's defeat of Akiyama at the age of 16 further cemented his status as an unusually talented young swordsman.[132] These awe-inspiring stories of Musashi's exploits traveled by

---

[126] Bennett, 64.
[127] Bennett, 64.
[128] Bennett, 65.
[129] Bennett, 65.
[130] Bennett, 65.
[131] Wilson, 193.
[132] Wilson, 175.

word of mouth, carried by those who retold the stories in action packed accounts to eager crowds in countless inns and drinking establishments throughout Japan. All who heard the tales were eager to hear more about this mysterious and unconventional swordsman.

Naturally, Musashi's fame reached even higher levels when news spread that he had single handedly defeated the entire Yoshioka Clan. The sensational nature of the duels and Musashi's skills were passed on not just to the warriors in martial arts schools, but also the peasants and merchants in the surrounding villages and towns. The story of a young man, barely 21, emerging out of obscurity and defeating the legendary Yoshioka Clan would have been juicy gossip even if it had not been true.[133] Thanks to these victories, Musashi's reputation increased exponentially, and his dramatic victory over the feared Sasaki Kojiro, combined with his strange state of dress and eccentric nature, only helped cement his status as a living legend.

When Musashi died in the summer of 1645, stories of his exploits had already been spread and embellished around Japan for decades. His life also coincided with new and exciting forms of entertainment in Japan, and given that Musashi represented a new type of hero for Japan, it only made sense that he would be featured in such artforms.

Less than 100 years after his death, Musashi's story had been made into kabuki, bunraku, and woodblock prints produced for the public, and by the beginning of the Meiji period (1868-1912), Musashi was depicted as the idealized version of samurai masculinity. The eccentric warrior possessed all the heroic qualities, and the Musashi legend would exemplify what one historian referred to as "a prescriptive representation of socially desirable ... institutions and ideas thought to have been handed down from generation to generation."[134] In the case of Musashi, this concept of invented tradition also connected directly to modern Japan's worries and desires about Japanese masculinity.

The legend of Musashi surged in the 20th century, as his story was depicted in various movies and books. Yoshikawa Eiji's popular 1935 novel about Musashi thoroughly captured the public's imagination, and in it Yoshikawa added to the Musashi legend by adapting the sword master's life to the *jidai shōsetsu*, a genre of popular literature that focused on idealized elements of courage, righteousness, and the martial prowess of historic male warriors. According to Ozaki Hotsuki, a specialist on the subject of *jidai shōsetsu,* this form of literature was known for its action, loose historical facts, conservative philosophy, and creative plotlines.[135] This literature genre was especially popular among the newly literate fiction readers who helped transform the commercial Japanese publishing industry in the 20th century.

---

[133] Wilson, 175.

[134] James R. Reichert, *Yoshikawa Eiji's Newspaper Novel Miyamoto Musashi, Gender, and Commercial Journalism*, (The Journal of Japanese Studies, vol. 44 no. 2, 2018), 296.

[135] Reichert, 296.

The legend of Musashi continued to spread in the late 20th century and early 21st century thanks to other depictions. *Vagabond* is a Japanese martial arts manga comic series written and illustrated by Takehiko Inoue. The manga is a fictionalized account of Musashi's life and heavily based on Yoshikawa's novel. *Vagabond* was published in 1998 with a total of 37 volumes by July 2014, and it won the 2000 Kodansha Manga Award and the 2002 Tezuka Osamu Cultural Prize. A huge hit, *Vagabond* has sold an astonishing 82 million copies around the world.

As Musashi's legacy spread, *The Book of Five Rings* was translated into multiple languages, and it continues to be read not only by people seeking martial arts knowledge, but also by those wishing to learn strategy and philosophy applicable to daily life and the business world. Furthermore, Musashi's experiences fighting in the wars of Japanese unification and his duels provide a direct link between the two important realms of the samurai experience: the battlefield and the duel. As such, his teachings on strategy and swordsmanship are still taught in modern kendo and martial arts.

While people continue to utilize Musashi's story and work for practical reasons, Musashi's legacy as a free thinking, unconventional warrior of incredible skill has captured the imaginations of generations of Japanese people. In countless books, comics, and movies, the image of the lone ronin samurai wandering throughout Japan on a masterless quest of martial arts perfection is a favorite character trope.

Musashi might have passed away nearly four centuries ago, but he is certain to live on through his own words and the stories told about him for several more centuries.

The grave marker for Musashi

The "Seishin Chokudo" monument in Kokura dedicated to Musashi

Online Resources

Other books about Japanese history by Charles River Editors

Other books about Musashi on Amazon

Further Reading

Bennett, Alexander C. "The Art of Living: EARLY MODERN KENJUTSU." *Kendo: Culture of the Sword*, 1st ed., University of California Press, Oakland, California, 2015, pp. 57–85.

Bennett, Alexander C. "The Art of Killing: SWORDSMANSHIP IN MEDIEVAL JAPAN." *Kendo: Culture of the Sword*, 1st ed., University of California Press, Oakland, California, 2015, pp. 26–56.

Blumberg, Arnold. "Between the 15th and Early 17th Centuries, Mounted Samurai Ruled Japan's Battlefields." *Military History*, vol. 21, no. 5, 12, 2004, pp. 28-78.

Birt, Michael P. "Samurai in Passage: The Transformation of the Sixteenth-Century Kanto." *Journal of Japanese Studies*, vol. 11, no. 2, 1985, pp. 369–399.

Bodart-Bailey, Beatrice M. "The First Year of Government." *The Dog Shogun: The Personality and Policies of Tokugawa Tsunayoshi*, University of Hawai'i Press, 2006, pp. 79–89.

Clulow, Adam. The Shogun's Loyal Vassals." *The Company and the Shogun: The Dutch Encounter with Tokugawa Japan*, Columbia University Press, 2014, pp. 95–132.

Farris, William Wayne. "Uneven Expansion in an Age of Endemic Warfare, 1450–1600." *Japan to 1600: A Social and Economic History*, University of Hawai'i Press, 2009, pp. 164–194.

Friday, Karl F. "Legacies of the Sword: The Kashima-Shinryu and Samurai Martial Culture," University of Hawai'i Press, 1997.

Hurst, Cameron G. "From Self-Protection to Self-Perfection in the Early and Mid Tokugawa." *Armed Martial Arts of Japan: Swordsmanship and Archery*, Yale University Press, 1998, pp. 53–81.

Hurst, Cameron. "The Early Tradition." *Armed Martial Arts of Japan: Swordsmanship and Archery*, Yale University Press, 1998, pp. 27–52.

Jaundrill, Colin D. "The Rise of 'Western' Musketry, 1841–1860." *Samurai to Soldier: Remaking Military Service in Nineteenth-Century Japan*, 1st ed., Cornell University Press, ITHACA; LONDON, 2016, pp. 13–46.

Matsunosuke, Nishiyama and Groemer Gerald. "EDO: THE WARRIOR'S CITY." *Edo Culture: Daily Life and Diversions in Urban Japan, 1600-1868*, University of Hawai'i Press, 1997, pp. 23–40.

Naohiro, Asao, and Marius B. Jansen. "Shogun and Tennō." *Japan Before Tokugawa: Political Consolidation and Economic Growth, 1500-1650*, edited by John Whitney Hall et al., Princeton University Press, 1981, pp. 248–270.

Pitelka, Morgan. "Severed Heads and Salvaged Swords: The Material Culture of War." *Spectacular Accumulation: Material Culture, Tokugawa Ieyasu, and Samurai Sociability*, University of Hawai'i Press, Honolulu, 2016, pp. 118–142.

Reichert, James R. "Yoshikawa Eiji's Newspaper Novel Miyamoto Musashi, Gender, and Commercial Journalism." *The Journal of Japanese Studies*, vol. 44 no. 2, 2018, p. 293-332.

Rogers, John M. "Arts of War in Times of Peace. Swordsmanship in Honcho Bugei Shoden, Chapter 6." *Monumenta Nipponica*, vol. 46, no. 2, 1991, pp. 173–202.

Silver, Alain. "SAMURAI." *Film Comment*, vol. 11, no. 5, 1975, pp. 10–15.

Suga, Takaaki. "Perceptions of Armor during the Edo Period." *Bulletin of the Detroit Institute of Arts*, vol. 88, no. 1/4, 2014, pp. 34–43.

Tokitsu, Kenji, "Miyamoto Musashi: His Life and Writings." Weatherhill, 2006.

Vaporis, Constantine Nomikos. "The Road to Edo (and Back)." *Tour of Duty: Samurai, Military Service in Edo, and the Culture of Early Modern Japan*, University of Hawai'i Press, 2008, pp. 36–61.

Varley, Paul. "The Country Unified." *Japanese Culture: Fourth Edition*, University of Hawai'i Press, 2000, pp. 140–163.

Wilson, William Scott, "The Lone Samurai: The Life of Miyamoto Musashi." Shambhala, 2013.

Free Books by Charles River Editors

We have brand new titles available for free most days of the week. To see which of our titles are currently free, click on this link.

Discounted Books by Charles River Editors

We have titles at a discount price of just 99 cents everyday. To see which of our titles are currently 99 cents, click on this link.